when spirits touch
duel poetry and photography
by Charles Martin & River Urke

when spirits touch
Copyright © 2013 by Charles Martin & River Urke

All rights reserved. No part of this publication may be reproduced, stored in a retrieval system, or transmitted by any means – electronic, mechanical, photographic (photocopying), recording, or otherwise – without prior permission in writing from the authors.

Printed in the United States of America

ISBN: 978-0615866604

Twowolvz Press
Stillwater, MN

cover by Charles Wm Martin

Dedicated

to

Poetic Voices Around the World

Table of Contents

Introduction 10

when the night winds blow 13

the passing 15

may we pray for you 17

stones 19

the path of wrath 21

morning prayer 23

the vanishing 25

when spirits touch 27

between our dawns 31

the gift 33

a winter's wind 35

down by the water's edge 37

teachings 38

a chalice of faith 40

illusion 43

the tear 44

their secret 45

when the guests leave 47

poetic strokes 49

freedom 51

gabriel *53*

Photography Credits ***55***

About the Authors ***56***
    Charles Martin 56
    River Maria Urke 57

CD –Voices of Poets ***59***

Introduction

"When power leads man towards arrogance, poetry reminds him of his limitations. When power narrows the area of man's concern, poetry reminds him of the richness and diversity of his existence. When power corrupts, poetry cleanses." John F. Kennedy

Each poet undertakes the process of writing poetry with the hopes of changing some aspect of life or conveying personal emotions which may facilitate understanding. It is most often a solitary undertaking. However, some poets have elected to join together to form a single creative voice often employing poetic forms adopted from Asia.

Duel Poetry is a prearranged poetry writing challenge between two poets to evolve a new free form poem based upon an initial prompt (4-5 lines) provided by one of the poets. Each writer in turn must respond to the other writer's lines (4 -5) until both parties agree that the poem is complete. The current volume of poetry represents three years of collaborative writing between River Urke and Charles Wm. Martin. The book illustrates what happens creatively when the spirits of two writers touch.

-Charles Wm Martin

when spirits touch

magic is born

Photography Credits page 55

when the night winds blow

when the night winds blow
and touch the heart of truth
what shall one do
hold it in a dream
until the moon rises full
and truth is revealed
or hide within the shadows
of pure denial
until the winds subside
and you hear your heart cry
longing to speak, hiding instead
knowing a bloom shall soothe
but the night bloom
fades in the light of day
its promise of truth
no more than a memory
a faded memory
only to return in dreams
silently waiting
for the next night bloom
but one moonless eve
the truth will not return
and the darkness
will cover your soul
attempting to spread
a thin layer of doubt
but entirely missing
a small flower of light
pulsing in the darkness
that begins to glow
pushing back the darkness
releasing your soul
as night blooms
you close your eyes
hesitant to know

the passing

you need not worry
for one day
i will not wake you
or
disrupt your dreams
when i curl next to you
in the night
for I will be a whisper
upon your silver tongue
a memory of another time
as I slip out before dawn
never to return as flesh
like a last breath
taken
but never
to return
I shall never
land
upon your shore again

may we pray for you

a life
a mere
drop in the bucket
of time
but to me
she was life
my life
swallowed whole
by the industry
she bled for
now she floats
barren in the universe
a token
of corporate greed
"may we pray for you"
a life
a mere moment in time
he joined for life
the gang to live
now she
is the price
of membership
a one-way ticket
but could he?
he has to
or he dies
his mama dies
Why?

stones

the rough edges
of the stone
have worn away
no longer does
its jagged edges
rip the flesh
from bone
it is not his tool
anymore
the stone moves on
with another story to tell
a story of rivers
rivers cutting deep
into the earth
smoothing stones
as if to end war
and she would
if a river had such power

the path of wrath

the molten steel
of this anger
flowed onto the plains
of his reason
scorching the fertile
ground of his thoughts
he falls to his knees
pain of the deepest slash
bleeds through tears
flooding him with despair
as his knees sink deep
into mother earth
he calls out for mercy
only to hear laughter
a sinister laugh of no other
than his wretched foe
the murderer of his love
sword in hand he took stance
facing empty air
the laughter reverberating
through the valley
cutting deeper into his moral soul
than any weapon could every do
he puts down his sword knowing
a battle will be his death
avenging his love is another way
he calls to his foe
you've murdered only one
of my two beloveds
i still have your wife's love
and she waits for me now
a flash of light explodes

knocking him down
tearing a hole in the earth
fuming with fury stands his foe
hands of attack they both roll
falling down to their deaths

morning prayer

tender are the memories
of your lips
against mine
warm is the touch
of hope
opening my eyes
each morning
as I wait for you
to return

Charlie Martin & River Urke

the vanishing

kneeling
in the sands
he waits
for
a drop of time
but found only
the dry bones
of yesterday
no future
no present
only
minute by
finished minute
of past moments
the bones
begin to cry
dry tears
empty of life
and true feelings
another masquerade
for god to see
or was it god
that took tomorrow
noticing people
don't seem to care
about the future

when spirits touch

the call of a lone wolf
echoes
through the deepest corners
of the northern forest
a sound so primeval
from a forgotten soul
a wanderer of time
a time before men
walked the mossy path
alone, separated
and divided from all
now their relative calls
out their names
pleading for them
to return to the old ways
when men knew their brothers
and walked with their sisters
a time they lived side by side
no blades between or
tar soaked earth
only the warmth of love
for one another
a deep respect
for all who shared this place
and walked upon this path
a thousand miles far
the call of a lone wolf
resonates, passing through
earth, water, fire, and air
a girl lifts her ears
and speaks to the wind

brother I hear you
your voice is my voice
your sadness is mine
the lone wolf replies
young one, I carry
too heavy a burden
for your soft back
the girl smiles
and says to the old one
then let us do as before
and share the burdens
of this world

between our dawns

write your name
on the shadows
in the corner
blow gentle thoughts
into the night wind
so that I might
feel you touch
the air between
our dawns
of time
I might
smell
your breath
in gentle rains
when passing
through the forest
or feel your flesh
next to mine
when I lie
upon the Earth
or let us take the risk
and wander
the garden
in-between
one last time
halfway
on the bridge
of tomorrows promises
and
today's lies
so that we might forget
the bitter taste
of betrayal
from broken rules
and families of honor
may love prevail

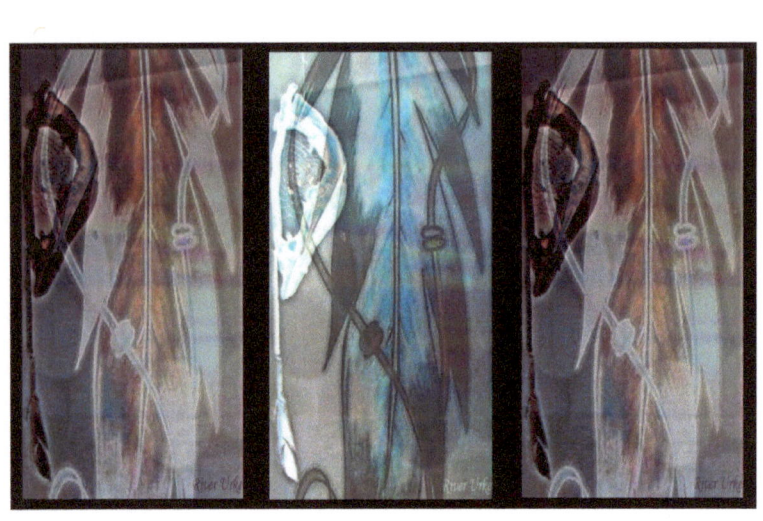

the gift

I dreamed a feather
fell from the hands
of my ancestors
landing at my feet
morphing into a shadow
a shadow of a soaring eagle
enveloping and lifting me
into the night sky
we flew for hours in silence
never sure
if I should be scared
or not
I questioned as I fought the pain
my bones shook
then he spoke to me by mind
saying with a voice
like a summers breeze
you needn't fear
I want only to show you
what was once ours
a garden of peace and light
as it once was
so you understand
why you must fight on
even when fear
wraps around your heart
keep moving forward
your ancestors are with you
the Eagle explains
gifting me a feather

a winter's wind

these things you hold so dear
cradled in your hands
as if a delicate bloom
are mere shadows of your past
you long to hold as it was
cradling a memory
framed in yesterday
unwilling to set him free
but he is not yours to hold
he belongs to a winter's wind
flowing through these barren trees
like his fingers once in your long hair
combing the woven threads of knowledge
the tangled web of life's intrinsic collective
delicately kissing a union of unattainable love
knowing he has to walk the paths not taken
your ache bears the weight of drowned tears
tears flowing from a thousand souls
abandoned by the gods of peace
and so each warrior must leave this place
and those he loves for one last futile battle
a battle of man against the natural world
a ludicrous yet crucial clash of power
he stands not with men ~horrified by
the hundreds of years of rape and pillage
leaving the earth a barren tract of sand
sand moving in the hour glass of history
though this narrow passage way of fate
to where his death will be found
the mere moment you know, stabbed
your heart bleeds for you and your unborn
a wail of agony escapes through silent cries
the loss of your beloved, her father
the time is here to set him free~
his soul flies with a winter's wind

down by the water's edge

a girl walks
along the fence
quietly
singing a tune
it is a song
she has heard
all of her life
from the wind
a song if sung
in the right place
at the right time
was pure magic
for hours of play
for butterflies
would dance
and
do somersaults
for the song
was pure love
alive
and
magic
was
in
the
air

teachings

the old man
opened his hand
and said
would you buy this
this emptiness
the young man
shook his head no
I would not buy
nothing
but
the old man said
each day
you buy

nothing
when you arise
expecting to live
throughout the day
but I give
thanks each morning I rise
the young man said
you taught me to pray
with asemaa to the new day
to be a giver
in this world of takers
you told me to watch
for what they will want
the old man said
your heard my words
but did not grasp
that even a warm hand
can cast a dark shadow
over the truth
no I did not, old man
I have to ask
how am I to know
truth
if all can be under shadow
the old man said
have you not seen
how the great owl
finds its prey
in the dark
with eyes
that question
all that it hears

a chalice of faith

one hundred lies
yellowed and torn
worn heavenly
by priests
and politicians
passing
by my door
wearing their lies
folded into crowns
crowns of greed
wrapped in deceit
bejeweled with the labors
of those easily deceived
those who believed
out of human fear
the fear that their lives
were nothing more
than unkept promises
they denied the visible
chose the mundane
persuaded fools
the pawns of the game
they are but
acceptable losses
in the campaign
for the holy grail of greed
a trickery of masked
crusades of destruction
illusions of truth
trapping the pawns
in a Gollum's trance

leaving them alone
quarreling with themselves
while the self-crowned nobility
quench their thirst
from a chalice
filled with the faith
of others

illusion

light
pierced
the darkness
beyond
his wave
of thought
a moment
long sought
but feared
for what
it might reveal
reality is
what it is not
the pendulum swings
striking crystal dreams
shattering hopes
and
fragmenting trust
to tiny bits of nothing
some will contemplate
while others continue
the illusion

the tear

they have stolen
the blanket from my
bed
the one i used
to wrap my child
up snug and tight
that one night last
winter
when the winds howled
and the storm took
what was left
of my frayed soul
my tears
mingling with the wind
and rain from hell
the land shook
with such fierce force
my child woke
in a daze
feverish and limp
with open eyes
revealing the sadness
of all mankind
and
a single tear
glistening
with the hope
for love

their secret

a dash of purples
and reds
a serenade of color
blends
in a boutique
greeting her
each morning
as she rises
a gift from god
for a moments time
a spiritual wave
for an agnostic mind
but feeling fades quickly
as she stares into
her child's eyes
and remembers
the pain of their days
his hand upon her cheek
her child screaming
no..........

when the guests leave

her heartbeat
drifts in the winds
above the border
a little girl
picks flowers
placing them
into neat piles
to sell to tourists
walking by
worlds removed
below the fading stars
it begins to rain
the tourists leave
the little girl makes
one last wreath
and places it upon
her mama's
roadside memorial

poetic strokes

she sat folded
in the nook of a tree
reading Neruda's words
sure that the scent
of lemons
were mingling with
cherry blossoms
opening before her eyes
in a glorious bloom
the wind lifts the petals
in a dance of poetry
free verse lines
vibrating across
the horizon's page
carefree and loved
unlike the life she lives
beyond the trees
her thirst for touch
rises her in flight
etching the day
upon a mirror
of yesterday
that now lies
shattered
reflecting only
pain
she looks away
and climbs down
tomorrows branch
surrounded in scents
and Neruda's words.

freedom

above the valley
of wild horses
a hawk soars the wind
calling your name
its voice echoes
through the valley
joining the river's song
asking you to return
home
come ride the red ridge
along the forgotten trail
of your grandfathers
free with mane in hand
touch the one soul
of all
who have passed
this way
and feel the heart beat
of time immortal
as thunder
rises through blades of gold
whispering secrets
forgotten
they gallop across
the prairie in between.

gabriel

beads tumble
down the crest
of the rising horn
skirts twirl
fingers tap
ancient rhythms
on sides of glasses
emotions liquid
beats flowing
among a purity of tone
a range of octaves
match the rising horn
then descending tones
passionate growls
bring wide-eyed smiles
and a chorus of sensual amens
a moment of silence
fills the room until
the ring of cymbals strike
as the music of soul
begins again

Imagination is Everything!

-Albert Einstein

Photography Credits

Page	Artist
12	Charles Martin
14	River Urke
16	Charles Martin
18	River Urke
20	Charles Martin
23	River Urke
24	Charles Martin
26	Charles Martin
29	River Urke
30	River Urke
32	River Urke
34	Charles Martin
36	River Urke
38	Charles Martin
40	Google Images
42	Charles Martin
44	Charles Martin
45	River Urke
46	Charles Martin
48	River Urke
50	River Urke
51	River Urke
52	Charles Martin

About the Authors

Charles Martin

CHARLES W. MARTIN (Reading Between the Minds [http://slpmartin.wordpress.com/]) -- earned his Ph.D. in Speech and Language Pathology with a minor in Statistics. Throughout Charlie's career as university professor, administrator, and Speech and Language Pathologist, he maintained a devotion to the arts (literature/poetry, the theater, music and photography). During that period he published poems in Ohio University Literary Magazine, Minority Voices: the Literary Magazine of the Pennsylvania State University, the Nebraska Literary Magazine, as well as in area newspapers. Since his retirement in 2010, he has turned his full attention to poetry and photography. He publishes a poem and a photographic art piece each day at Read Between the Minds. He is noted as a poet  of social conscience. Charlie has been blogging since January 31, 2010. He has recently released a self-published book of poetry entitled The Hawk Chronicles and will soon publish another book called A Bea in Your Bonnet: First Sting, featuring the renowned Aunt Bea. In The Hawk Chronicles, Charlie provides a personification of his resident hawk with poems and photos taken over a two-year period. His photography has been purchased for a number of private collections in Southern California.

River Maria Urke

River has the heart of a poet and the eyes of an artist. She sees the world through a lens of creation filtered through imagination. Her poetic writings and artistic touches reflect her Ojibwe and Celtic heritages along with her ponderings being a thirty something American mother. She lives in the St Croix Valley of Minnesota with her daughter Willow and her boyfriend Tommy.

River's first publication, *Stumbled & Standing*, is a collection of poetry and essay focused on life with Multiple Sclerosis. Her second publication, *Womens Obsession with Shoes*, is a creative book of memoirs by women about life through a pair of shoes. River is a member of the Mulberry Street Poets in Stillwater and the TGI Frybread poetry group in Minneapolis.

website: http://www.rivermaria.com/

CD –Voices of Poets

Optional CD Accompanied Audio Recorded poetry reading

with

Charles Martin and River Urke,

with special guests:

Liliana Negoi,

David J. Bauman,

JohnnyK,

Tommy Blackwolf,

Susie Clevenger

www.ingramcontent.com/pod-product-compliance
Lightning Source LLC
Chambersburg PA
CBHW041403090426
42743CB00006B/145